Inside the World's Most Infamous Terrorist Organizations

Hamas
Palestinian Terrorists

Maxine Rosaler

The Rosen Publishing Group, Inc.
New York

Published in 2003 by The Rosen Publishing Group, Inc.
29 East 21st Street, New York, NY 10010

Library of Congress Cataloging-in-Publication Data

Rosaler, Maxine.
Hamas: Palestinian terrorists / Maxine Rosaler.— 1st ed.
    p. cm.— (Inside the world's most infamous terrorist organizations)
Summary: Discusses the origins, philosophy, and most notorious
attacks of the Hamas terrorist group, including their present activities,
possible plans, and counter-terrorism efforts directed against them.
Includes bibliographical references and index.
ISBN 0-8239-3820-4 (lib. bdg.)
1. Harakat al-Muqawamah al-Islamiyah. 2. Terrorism—Palestine. 3.
Arab-Israeli conflict. 4. Palestinian Arabs—Warfare. [1. Hamas.
2. Terrorism—Palestine. 3. Arab-Israeli conflict. 4. Palestinian Arabs.]
I. Title. II. Series.
HV6433.P252 H377 2003
956.9405'4—dc21

2002007769

Manufactured in the United States of America

Contents

Introduction

Downtown Jerusalem is deserted, with stores and restaurants closing down daily for lack of business. The reason? Deadly attacks by the Palestinian terrorist group Hamas that occur with numbing regularity. Cafés and restaurants, the favored targets of Palestinian suicide bombers, are posting security guards at their doors. Some Israelis have taken to wearing bullet-proof vests when they venture downtown. Most residents, however, are choosing to stay home.

"It's getting more and more scary," says Sarah Shapiro, an American-born writer who has been living in Israel for the past twenty-six years, in an interview with the author. "The normal feeling of human beings is usually that it won't happen to me. Now the feeling is more and more, 'How could it not happen to me? How long can my luck hold out?'

"Everyone knows someone who has been killed or hurt," she continues, telling of the classmate of her seventeen-year-old daughter, a casualty of a recent attack who has been lying in a hospital bed, brain dead, for the past year and a half. Shapiro tells of a woman she knows whose daughter was killed, and who will not come out of her house anymore. "She won't talk to anyone, she's so devastated. She won't go anywhere. She's totally gone." Overprotectiveness and seclusion are common responses of parents whose children have been victims of terrorism, she says, explaining that she has forbidden her own children to visit downtown Jerusalem.

An ultra-orthodox Jew walks in the Mahane Yehuda market in Jerusalem on April 13, 2002, near the site of a suicide bombing that had occurred that day. A female Palestinian bomber killed six Israelis and wounded sixty when she blew herself up at a bus stop outside a crowded open-air market. Beginning in early 2002, female suicide bombers began to appear in Israel, a departure from the standard profile of the young male Palestinian bomber.

Hamas (Arabic for "zeal" or "religious passion") is accomplishing what it set out to achieve when it began its terrorist attacks against the Israeli people over twenty years ago. First established in 1978 as a Palestinian social services organization, it has grown into one of the most lethal forces of terrorism in Israel today. Hamas's immediate goal is to disrupt the peace process between Israel and

An Israeli explosives expert examines a car that exploded minutes before in West Jerusalem on April 1, 2002. A Palestinian bomber blew himself up in the attack near the Old City of Jerusalem, critically wounding a policeman who stopped the bomber's car at a roadblock.

the Palestinian people (and the Arab world at large). Its larger goal, however, is the destruction of Israel. It seeks to achieve these goals by perpetuating an endless cycle of violence that will chase the Israelis from the land Hamas considers to be Palestinian and spark an Israeli retaliation that will create a wider Arab-Israeli war. It hopes that this war will leave Palestinians in sole possession of the land Israel now occupies.

Hamas reasons that by committing acts of violence against Israel, Israeli citizens will oppose and distrust any possibility of making permanent peace with the Palestinians. In addition, it will force Israel's leaders to retaliate against the Palestinians. And, indeed, Israel responds to Hamas violence by attacking terrorist sites located in Palestinian villages and refugee camps and rooting out terrorists, in the process often destroying homes and stores, disrupting schools and businesses, and, occasionally, accidentally killing people. Israeli operatives have even assassinated suspected terrorist leaders. All of this serves to further inflame Palestinian anger against Israelis, who are viewed as an occupying force. Ordinary Palestinians take to the streets and clash violently with the Israeli military, while Hamas uses Israeli retaliation as an excuse to escalate its terrorist attacks and spark a larger war that they hope will result in the total destruction of the state of Israel.

So, with each Hamas bombing and Israeli retaliation, the cycle of violence is perpetuated, and the goal of many Palestinians and Israelis for peaceful coexistence recedes ever further into the distance.

A Land Divided

The area that is now home to the Palestinians and Israelis was, in biblical times, known as Canaan. Hebrew tribes first began moving into it around 1225 BC after fleeing slavery in Egypt and conquering the Canaanites. Around 1050 BC, a very war-like people, the Philistines (after whom Palestine would later be named), invaded the Hebrew lands but were eventually beaten back, and the nation of Israel began to grow and stabilize.

A series of invasions and exiles, however, between 586 BC and AD 638 would eventually force nearly all Jews away from the land they considered to be promised to them by God. These exiled Jews became known as the Diaspora (the Greek word for dispersion).

Seeking a homeland that would offer them a refuge from persecution after years of wandering in unwelcoming countries, Jews began returning to Palestine in the 1800s. This desire of Jews to return to the original site of the Israel of biblical times was called Zionism (named after Sion, a citadel, or fortress, that was the heart of biblical Jerusalem).

Modern Israel and Palestine

The aftermath of World War II would provide the Zionist movement with a new sense of urgency. After six million Jews were killed in Europe during the Nazi Holocaust, Jews felt the need for their own state more than ever. They wanted to have a refuge from persecution, where all Jews would be welcome and strongly defended. Before and during the war, very few European countries accepted Jewish refugees fleeing Adolf Hitler, and those that did generally accepted very few. After the war, there were over 100,000 survivors of the Holocaust living in European displaced-persons camps, with no homes to return to and nowhere else to go.

Many of these refugees wished to settle in Palestine, which was then controlled by the British. The British refused, on the grounds that it was confronting armed rebellions of Arab and Jewish groups fighting for control of Palestine. Both Jews and Arabs engaged in terrorist attacks against the British that included kidnappings, sabotage, and bombings.

No longer willing to commit so many troops and so much money to the "Palestinian problem," the British authorized the United Nations (UN) to draft a solution. On November 29, 1947, the UN passed a resolution that divided Palestine into three parts: an Arab state, a Jewish state, and Jerusalem, which would have "international status" and be shared by both Arabs and Jews.

This apparent breakthrough was short-lived, however. The Arabs rejected the resolution after it was passed, setting off a wave of violence between Arabs and Jews throughout Palestine. Arabs had opposed the Zionist movement from the start, regarding it as a threat to their own desire for a Palestinian state. At the time of the UN resolution, the Jewish population in Palestine was 600,000, and the Palestinian population was 1.3 million. Both the Jews and the Palestinians believed they had an exclusive right to the entire territory known as Palestine, and both considered it to be the site of their heritage. Each regarded the other as usurpers (someone who steals something that belongs to someone else).

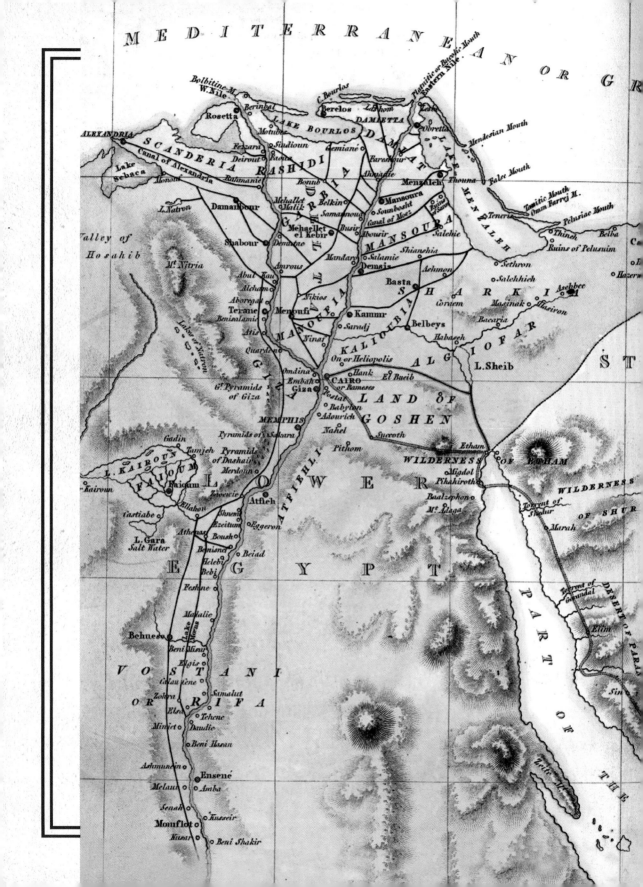

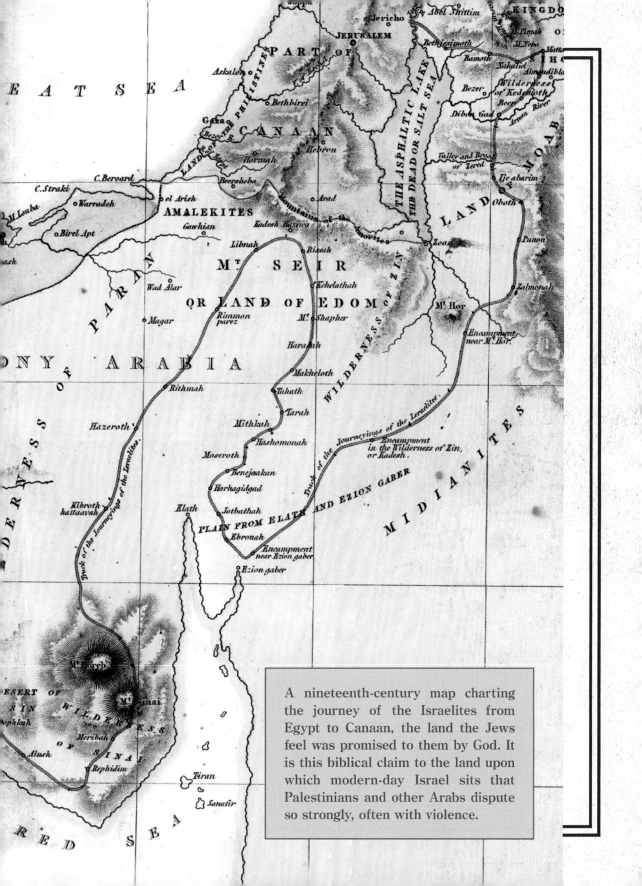

A nineteenth-century map charting the journey of the Israelites from Egypt to Canaan, the land the Jews feel was promised to them by God. It is this biblical claim to the land upon which modern-day Israel sits that Palestinians and other Arabs dispute so strongly, often with violence.

Yet the Israelis accepted the terms of the UN resolution, which they said was "the indispensable minimum." The Arabs rejected it forcefully.

Reacting to Arab Palestinian violence, on May 14, 1948, David Ben-Gurion, head of a militant Zionist group, proclaimed the establishment of the State of Israel, and he became its first prime minister. Within a year, fifty-three nations officially recognized the new nation, and the UN offered it membership in May 1949.

Only one day after Ben-Gurion declared the establishment of Israel, Arab military forces invaded the new nation. The fighters included Egyptians, Iraqis, Jordanians, Syrians, Lebanese, Saudi Arabians, and Yemenis. Most of these troops were poorly trained, ill-equipped, and very inexperienced, while Israeli forces included 20,000 to 25,000 WWII veterans. The Israelis gained a decisive victory. By January 1949, Israel held an area that was considerably larger than the area assigned to it by the UN partition plan. The only parts of Palestine that remained in Arab hands were the West Bank (annexed, or incorporated, into its own country by Jordan) and the Gaza Strip (held by Egypt). Jerusalem was divided between the Arab and Jewish populations, rather than jointly held and administered. The Old City, the Western Wall, and the site of Solomon's Temple (upon which stands a Muslim mosque called the Dome of the Rock) were held by the Jordanians. Israel possessed the New City.

The UN organized a cease-fire in the summer of 1948, and truce agreements between the Israelis and the various Arab countries were completed by July of 1949. The land held by the Jordanians and Egyptians after the 1948 war would remain under their control until June 1967.

Arab prisoners at the Egyptian fortress overlooking the Strait of Tiran, on June 12, 1967, soon after its capture by Israeli forces following the Six Day War with Egypt, Jordan, and Syria. The Strait of Tiran is a strategic and important shipping channel above the Gulf of Aqaba that sits between the Sinai Peninsula on the west and Saudi Arabia on the east. Egypt's president, Gamal Abdel Nasser, had blockaded the strait, cutting off Israel's access to the Red Sea and beyond. One of the results of the Six Day War was to break this blockade and allow Israeli shipping to resume.

The 1967 War

In 1967, the Arab countries surrounding Israel prepared to stage a massive attack against it. Armies from three neighboring countries—Egypt, Jordan, and Syria—began amassing armies at the borders. Israel launched a preemptive strike against these armies (a surprise attack designed to prevent enemy strikes).

In just six days, Israel won the 1967 war, which became known as the Six Day War. As a consequence of this war, Israel acquired more land, including the West Bank, Golan Heights, the Gaza Strip, the Sinai Peninsula, and the eastern half of Jerusalem.

At first, the Six Day War seemed to be a huge victory for Israel. Its new territory seemed to provide a buffer from further Arab attacks and invasions. But possessing this land simply multiplied the barriers to peace that already existed long before 1967.

Israeli Settlement

The 1967 war left Israel in control of over two million Arabs who had been living in Palestine at the time. Israel proceeded to bring armies in to police the territory it had acquired. While Israel said that it was necessary to maintain a military presence on these lands in order to protect itself from future attacks, the Arabs said that the Israeli occupation was just a pretext for annexing the land (incorporating another country or territory into one's own). These newly acquired lands became known to Palestinians and their supporters as the occupied territories.

Israelis proceeded to move into these captured lands and build new communities, or settlements, on them. Israel contended that since no one had legal rights to this land (both Arabs and Jews laid claim to it), and since it had been acquired during a just war, Israelis had just as much right to settle there as the Palestinians. Furthermore, Israel stated that since Jews had lived on some of this land as far back as biblical times, they had previous rights to it. They also pointed out that some of the land under dispute, such as the city of Hebron, had been the sites of Arab massacres of large numbers of Jews. Arabs, on the other hand, saw the building of Jewish settlements as part of a strategy of slowly driving them out of the occupied territories.

Israeli armed patrols on the narrow walled streets of Jerusalem during the Six Day War in June 1967. This sort of military presence in Jerusalem and in the territories captured during the war would stoke the bitter fire of Palestinian anger and resentment, leading twenty years later to the first large-scale explosion of organized rebellion against Israeli occupation—the First Intifada of 1987.

The legacy of the 1967 war—Israeli settlement and occupation of the West Bank and Gaza Strip—is the source of much of the tension between Israel and the Palestinians today.

The First Intifada

During the period after the 1967 war, Israel continued to maintain a military presence on the land it had acquired during that war and subsequent conflicts with its Arab neighbors. The Palestinian people resented the presence of Israeli soldiers on what they considered to be their homeland. Throughout this period, Arabs, mostly

Jerusalem

The failure of Arabs and Jews to agree over the future status of Jerusalem is a major source of tension between Israel and the Palestinians. Israel wants total control over Jerusalem, while Palestinians want authority over East Jerusalem. The ancient city has great historical and religious significance for both Israelis and Palestinians, most of whom are Muslims. For Muslims, it is the site of the al-Aqsa Mosque, the site from which Muslims believe the prophet Mohammed, the founder of Islam, flew up to Heaven. For Jews, it is the site of the temple that King Solomon built to house the Ark of the Covenant (a sacred container for the stone tablets bearing the Ten Commandments given by God to Moses, an early leader of the Jews). The Western Wall is all that remains of that temple. Also called the Wailing Wall, it is the most sacred Jewish shrine, a place where Jews from around the world gather to pray and lament.

under the direction of the Palestine Liberation Organization (PLO) and its leader, Yasir Arafat, staged guerrilla attacks on Israel to express their resentment over the Israeli occupation.

The resentment of the Palestinian people continued to build and fester until, in December 1987, it exploded in what is known as the First Intifada (*intifada* is the Arabic word for "uprising"). The intifada consisted of mass protests, most of them nonviolent, in the form of strikes, boycotts of Israeli products, and other acts of civil disobedience.

The intifada had broken out spontaneously, and Hamas, which up until then had been essentially a social services organization

A parade of a futuwa (guerrilla) unit trained by the Palestinian Liberation Army (PLA) in the Israeli desert in 1967. The PLA was formed in 1964 as the military arm of the Palestine Liberation Organization (PLO), an umbrella group for various Palestinian factions and resistance groups. Until the Six Day War of 1967, the PLA was based in Gaza and had links to the Egyptian government. Under PLO leader Yasir Arafat, the PLA followed a strategy of guerrilla warfare with forces deployed in Syria, Lebanon, and a few units in the West Bank and Gaza Strip.

(providing assistance to impoverished Palestinians), proceeded to take a more active role in escalating the level of protest. Hamas activists handed out leaflets and made fiery speeches, encouraging Palestinians to more violent forms of protest. Teenagers set fire to tires in order to block off traffic intersections, and old women and children would collect stones to throw at Israeli soldiers. Hamas also supplied the Palestinian youths with Molotov cocktails, a primitive kind of firebomb.

During the intifada, Hamas distributed leaflets urging a "revolution of knives" and calling for the use of guns against Israeli security personnel and civilians. These leaflets, which referred to Jews as "the offspring of apes and pigs," incited riots and attacks against Israeli soldiers and civilians alike. Almost all of the leaflets ended with a call for "jihad [holy war] until victory, or martyrdom for the sake of Allah [God]."

Origins of Hamas

Until the intifada of 1987, Hamas had been primarily involved in providing social services to the Palestinians, such as welfare support, charitable services, and education. At the time of its creation in 1978, Israeli officials viewed it as a welcome alternative to the PLO, which during the 1970s and 1980s was the major terrorist organization operating in Israel, the West Bank, and Gaza Strip.

Hamas, whose ideals were deeply rooted in Islamic fundamentalism, was strongly opposed to the PLO because the PLO was a secular organization, meaning that religion was not central to its goals. The fact that Hamas was opposed to the PLO was something that the Israelis welcomed. Its perspective was, "The enemy of my enemy is my friend"—little realizing how fiercely this "friendship" of convenience would sour.

Publicly, Hamas appeared to be solely interested in serving the Palestinian community's spiritual and social needs. Its leaders preached sermons that promised religious salvation from the poverty and despair that were prevalent throughout the Palestinian community. Rather than criticize the Israeli occupation, they instead encouraged their followers to focus on spiritual matters.

Israeli officials welcomed the fact that Hamas was a religious organization that promoted the spread of Islam. In the late 1970s and early 1980s, terrorist groups had not yet started to use Islam as a justification for violence. In the view of the Israeli establishment, promoting religion seemed to serve the purpose of quelling Palestinian unrest.

With this Israeli support, membership in Hamas continued to grow. Israel was unaware that Hamas had developed a secret political agenda and that it was engaging in covert activities. Hamas began establishing small groups, or cells, that were stockpiling weapons and ammunition in hiding places throughout the Gaza Strip for eventual use against Israeli targets. Hamas's active role in inciting violence was finally revealed during the First Intifada, leading Israel to ban the organization in 1989. Around this time Israel also discovered a cache of weapons in the home of Hamas spiritual leader Ahmed Yassin.

In the late 1980s and early 1990s, Hamas violence escalated to a new level that included drive-by shootings, kidnappings, and ambushes and murders of Israeli soldiers and Shin Bet (Israeli secret police) agents. In 1992, Hamas established its military wing, the Izzedine al Qassam Brigade, thus marking its official emergence as a terrorist organization.

Hamas Ideology

Hamas's short-term aim is complete Israeli withdrawal from the West Bank and Gaza Strip. After the 1948 war, only 170,000 of the 800,000 Arabs living in Palestine remained in the territories that became Israel. The rest became refugees in neighboring Arab nations. No

The founder of Hamas, Sheikh Ahmed Yassin, in his home in the Gaza Strip, March 14, 2002. Once supported by the Israeli government for its efforts to minister to the spiritual needs of Palestinians, Hamas was outlawed once it became apparent that it was stockpiling weapons and ammunition and encouraging Palestinians to resist Israeli occupation with violence.

Arab state would accept them as citizens but instead placed them in refugee camps. These refugees began to fight to return to their former homes by staging guerrilla attacks on Israel. One of Hamas's demands is that all these Palestinians be allowed to return to their homes in the territory currently occupied by Israel. Since this would result in Palestinians greatly outnumbering the Jews, Israel says that allowing the refugees to return would be "political suicide."

Hamas's long-term aim, however, is far more ambitious and even more deadly. It wants to eliminate Israel and Jews altogether and establish a Muslim fundamentalist religious state on the land the Koran (the Muslim holy book) claims for followers of Islam—the territory stretching from the Mediterranean Sea to the Jordan River, land which currently contains the entire state of Israel. Hamas hopes that its terrorist attacks will eventually succeed in making life so dangerous and frightening for Israelis that living on that land will become unbearable.

The Issues

Hamas gives a voice to many Palestinians, who resent the restrictions that the Israeli occupation puts on their lives. As Hassan Abdel Rahman, a PLO official, put it in an interview on *The NewsHour with Jim Lehrer*, Israeli occupation "confiscates Palestinian freedom, dignity, and doesn't allow them to develop as a free people in their own country."

Under occupation, Palestinians wanting to travel within and between parts of the West Bank and Gaza Strip are subjected to a complicated system of ID cards, travel permits, and checkpoints. During periods of increased violence, Israel imposes additional restrictions. These restrictions include cutting the Palestinian territories off from Israel through the establishment of barricades and roadblocks. Barricades prevent Palestinian teachers and students from reaching classes taught in Israeli territory. Barricades also prevent Palestinian residents of the territories from going to their jobs in Israel. This results in widespread unemployment and poverty among the Palestinians.

Israel's Neighbors

While there has been conflict between Israel and its neighbors for thousands of years, there have been times when both parties have agreed to sign truces. When truces break down, all-out warfare often results. In addition to the 1948 and 1967 wars, Israel has had the following military conflicts with its Arab neighbors:

The Sinai Campaign: 1956
In response to Egypt blocking Israel's access to the Suez Canal and continued attacks against Israeli communities, Israel invaded the Egyptian-controlled Sinai Peninsula. Following a cease-fire, the UN took control of the area.

The Yom Kippur War: 1973
With the support of other Arab states, Egypt and Syria attacked Israel during the Jewish holy day of Yom Kippur. Israel succeeded in pushing them back.

The Lebanon War: 1982
In an effort to end PLO raids from Lebanon into Israel, Israel attacked Beirut and southern Lebanon. The PLO agreed to leave Beirut and move its headquarters to Tunisia.

In addition, Israel often responds militarily to Hamas terrorism, sending soldiers, tanks, and fighter jets into the West Bank and Gaza Strip. The wave of Hamas suicide bombings in Israel in March and April of 2002 (which killed several dozen Israeli civilians) prompted the most massive Israeli military response since the 1967 war. In its attempt to root out Hamas terrorists, the Israeli army destroyed

Palestinians inspect the ruins of a building used as a hideout by Hamas activists and damaged during an Israeli army incursion into the northern West Bank town of Nablus on May 3, 2002. An Israeli soldier and a Hamas member were killed during the pre-dawn military operation.

many homes, offices, and stores; made Arafat a prisoner within his surrounded enclave; assassinated a key Hamas leader, Sheikh Salah Shehada, and killed many Palestinians caught in the crossfire. This kind of aggressive Israeli military reaction, though justified in many people's eyes, is yet another reason for Palestinian resentment (not to mention international concern). It seems sure to breed a new generation of Palestinian terrorists among the Arabs, who will become a part of this endless series of attacks and counterattacks.

— Inside Hamas —

In 1994, with the bombing of a bus in the Israeli town of Afula, Hamas began launching its most lethal form of attack: the suicide bombing. After a lull in terrorist activities during part of 1995, Hamas resumed launching suicide attacks in Israel in 1996, at a level never before seen. This pattern of escalation and retreat was followed throughout the next several years, revealing the full extent of the anger and hatred felt by many Palestinians toward Israelis—a burning hatred carefully fostered by Hamas.

The Sbarro Bombing

In August 2001, Hamas terrorist activities reached a level of violence previously unseen when a suicide bomber blew himself up in a Sbarro pizzeria in downtown Jerusalem, killing fifteen people, including several children.

Many attacks preceded the Sbarro bombing, and many have followed it, some of which have resulted in even higher Israeli casualties. Still, the Sbarro bombing seems to stick in the minds of many Israelis as the event that first brought the real threat of terrorism home to them in a very direct, immediate way.

"Sbarro was a part of our lives," says Sarah Shapiro. She goes on to recall how Sbarro was where her children and their friends used to go on weekends and after school, and where her daughter celebrated her twelfth birthday. "After Sbarro, it seems that there

CHAPTER

2

Israeli police and volunteers inspect the scene of a suicide bombing that killed fifteen people and wounded more than eighty others at a Sbarro pizzeria on August 9, 2001. Up to that time, it had been the worst bombing in Jerusalem since the beginning of a Palestinian uprising in September 2000.

is nowhere that is safe anymore. Every time I say good-bye to my children in the morning, I'm scared," she says.

Hamas said that the Sbarro bombing, and a string of bombings that preceded and followed it, were in retaliation for Israel's assassination of several of the group's leaders. It is also no coincidence that the peace process had been revived before the bombing, an effort that Hamas violently opposes. Perhaps more than any other previous attack, the Sbarro bombing opened Israeli eyes to the danger Hamas represented and the murderous sway it held over its members.

How Palestinians View Hamas Attacks

While people around the world regard attacks like the one on Sbarro as terrorism, Palestinians see them as acts of resistance or martyrdom. They feel that since Israel is a foreign power occupying their territory, they have a right to fight to liberate their homeland. Some are willing to offer an end to terrorist attacks in exchange for regaining possession and authority over the West Bank, Gaza Strip, and East Jerusalem (this is known as the "land for peace" formula). Other Palestinians feel that both sides must renounce violence and arrive at a negotiated settlement that will foster trust and cooperation between the two neighbors.

Children of Hamas

Starting from an early age, some Palestinian children are taught to hate Israel in particular and Jews in general. Hamas accomplishes this by running schools that teach Hamas philosophy and beliefs to impressionable young minds.

Textbooks in these schools state that Israel is evil. On maps of the region, the name "Palestine" covers the entire region that Israel currently occupies. In many cases, young Palestinians are urged by their schools, media, clerics, and political leaders to someday do their part to destroy Israel. Children are taught that the "treacherous" Jews have no historical or religious ties to Jerusalem or any part of Israel.

An important function of these Hamas schools is to groom children to be suicide bombers. Signs posted on the walls of their kindergartens read, "The children of the kindergarten are the shaheeds [holy martyrs] of tomorrow." "We like to grow them," Hamas leader Sheik Hasan Yosef told *USA Today*. "From kindergarten through college."

A Palestinian boy holds a toy gun during a September 2001 Hamas rally supporting suicide bomb attacks against Israel at the Al Noserate refugee camp in the southern Gaza Strip. Some Palestinian children are taught from a very early age to hate Jews and devote themselves to the effort to destroy the state of Israel.

Palestinian girls chant anti-Israeli slogans during a Hamas march in the Jabalya refugee camp in the northern Gaza Strip in April 2002. More than 15,000 people marched in the camp in support of the continuation of the uprising against Israeli occupation of the West Bank and Gaza Strip.

"You don't start educating a shaheed at age twenty-two," Roni Shaked, an Israeli journalist who specializes in writing about terrorism, told *USA Today*. "You start at kindergarten, so by the time he's twenty-two, he's looking for an opportunity to sacrifice his life."

An eleven-year-old Palestinian student named Ahamed gives chilling testimony to the effectiveness of Hamas's plan. "I will

Mothers of Hamas Members

The goal of the Hamas schools is to create future suicide bombers, and difficult as it is to comprehend, many mothers of Hamas students dream of the day their children will sacrifice their lives to kill Jews and become martyrs for the Palestinian cause. This shocking death wish is in great part due to the very low quality of life that most Palestinians have. Many Palestinians think that, when all they see around them is violence, poverty, and lack of opportunity, they don't have much of a chance of living a long and happy life. What is there to live for, they ask? For example, Najwa Amarneh, a thirty-three-year-old mother of three, hopes that her son, Mohammed, who is now four, will one day give his life to the Palestinian struggle. "My son is still young, but in the future, God willing, he will be first a fighter, then a martyr," she told the *Boston Globe*. "As a mother, this is not a good thing. Everyone likes his life and his children's lives. But our life here is a test and is short. The next life is better." She points out proudly that even now, at the age of four, her son Mohammed "wants to buy a pistol to kill all Jews."

make my body a bomb that will blast the flesh of Zionists, the sons of pigs and monkeys," he told *USA Today*. "I will tear their bodies into little pieces and cause them more pain than they will ever know."

This Hamas-sponsored education in hatred and terror continues on right through university. Classroom signs at Al-Najah University in the West Bank city of Nablus and at Gaza's Islamic University read, "Israel has nuclear bombs, we have human bombs."

Structure of Hamas

In order to create the kind of passion and loyalty necessary to sustain an intifada and wave after wave of suicide bombings, Hamas has developed an elaborate structure that allows it to influence virtually every corner of Palestinian life. Hamas makes certain to leave no segment of the Palestinian population untouched. It reaches into the hearts, minds, and souls of Palestinians, hoping to control the practical details of their daily lives and buy their long-term support and loyalty. This enables Hamas to create an endless supply of people who can help it achieve its goals.

As an organization, Hamas is composed of several different parts. Some parts work in secret (covertly), while others operate out in the open (overtly). The open activities include a political division, which is responsible for recruiting members and spreading propaganda. Hamas also operates a vast social services network, which provides a host of charity, welfare, and aid services to the Palestinian community.

Much of Hamas's funding comes from other countries. Hamas uses its social activities as a pretext for raising funds for its terrorist activities. In December 2001, the administration of United States president George W. Bush, as part of its war on terrorism following the attacks of September 11, 2001, froze the assets of the Holy Land Foundation, the largest Muslim charity in the United States, for allegedly funding Hamas. As reported by *NewsHour*, President Bush said that Holy Land was not a legitimate charity since it supported the building of schools to "indoctrinate children to grow up into suicide bombers" and supported the bombers' families after deadly suicide missions.

The social services network and the political division provide cover for militant activity, and these two divisions—and their funding—support Hamas terrorism in a number of ways.

Overt and Covert Activities

Hamas's social services help make Hamas popular with the Palestinian people, who are grateful for the much-needed help the organization offers them. Hamas builds schools, mosques, and hospitals in the territories and provides a number of essential welfare services to the impoverished Palestinian community. Some of these services are directed specifically to the families of suicide bombers, who receive from Hamas money, housing, and the glory and honor of having a relative who has martyred himself for the Palestinian cause. Hamas officials working in the political and social services divisions of the organization routinely deny any connection to the military brigades.

The al-Qassam Brigade is Hamas's military wing. It operates entirely in secret and is currently believed to include up to 500 young volunteers preparing for suicide missions. It is organized into many small, self-contained cells whose mission is to carry out terrorist activities. If the leader of one cell is killed, or even if an entire cell is eliminated, another leader or cell can quickly be called in as a replacement. The other advantage of a cell structure is that, in the event of being captured, members of one cell can not reveal the secret plans of other cells under interrogation. Each cell is only aware of its own assigned activities.

The Suicide Bombers

T he spring of 1994 marked a turning point in Hamas history. This was when it adopted the suicide bombing strategy, its most deadly and now most popular and effective form of attack. These bombings marked a major escalation in Hamas's commitment to violence and its ability to instill almost constant fear in the hearts and minds of Israeli citizens.

How Suicide Bombing Became a Tactic

Hamas's decision-making process behind adopting suicide bombings as a terrorist tactic against Israeli occupation is shrouded in mystery. The suicide bombing campaign is generally thought to have been inspired by two very different events—an act of war and a brief moment of peace. They were masterminded by the most unlikely of terrorist figures—a soft-spoken Palestinian engineer.

The Hebron Massacre

Before sunrise on February 25, 1994, an American-born Israeli doctor and Orthodox Jew, Baruch Goldstein, shot and killed 29 Palestinians and wounded 150 while they were praying in a mosque located in the town of Hebron on the West Bank. The massacre outraged and sickened Palestinians and Israelis alike, but it is thought that this terrorist attack, perpetrated by an Israeli, provoked a "fight fire with fire" response among Palestinian militants. In a sense, it provided militants with a justification for the suicide bombings that followed.

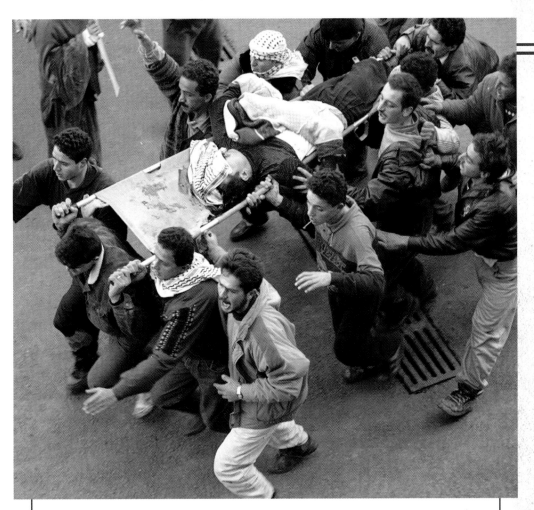

Palestinians rush a seriously wounded man to a hospital in the West Bank city of Hebron. He was shot in rioting that followed the Hebron Massacre of February 25, 1994. In this attack, an American-born Israeli doctor, Baruch Goldstein, killed twenty-nine Muslim worshippers and wounded 150 others in Hebron's Cave of the Patriarch Mosque. The massacre was believed to be the bloodiest attack on Palestinians since Israel seized the West Bank and Gaza Strip following the Six Day War of 1967.

Goldstein was said to have been upset the night before, after Muslims shouted "Slaughter the Jews" during prayer services he was attending. In addition, as a doctor who had treated many victims of terrorism over the years, he was increasingly angered and disgusted by the Intifada-related violence.

The Oslo Accords

One reason that was given for Goldstein's massacre was his opposition to the Oslo Accords. In the Oslo Accords, Israel had agreed to give territory back to the Palestinians in exchange for the Palestinian leader Yasir Arafat's promise that he would crack down on terrorism. It was Goldstein's feeling that Israeli prime minister Yitzhak Rabin was giving up too much in the agreement.

The Oslo Accords were also a source of contention for Hamas. One of the primary founding principles of Hamas is that peace with Israel is not only undesirable, but impossible. The September 1993 signing of the Oslo Accords indicated that peace with Israel might be on the horizon.

Furthermore, in the Oslo Accords, Yasir Arafat recognized Israel's right to exist. This was enough to enrage hardline Palestinian militants. Hamas has never wavered in its belief that all of the land that Israel occupies belongs to the Palestinians and the Palestinians alone: None of it belongs to Israel, not even the portion originally offered to it under the UN partition resolution of 1947. Arafat's recognition of Israel first as a nation, and second as a nation permitted to exist on Palestinian land, went against everything that Hamas stood for.

Reduced Israeli Oversight

In addition to motivating Hamas to escalate its terrorism, the Oslo Accords also laid the groundwork that made such escalation physically possible. Part of the Oslo Accords included an agreement by Israel to give up its right to search out and attack terrorists in the West Bank and Gaza Strip before they struck. Under the accords, Israel had agreed that Yasir Arafat, the Palestinian leader with

Palestinian leader Yasir Arafat escorts Leah Rabin, wife of assassinated Israeli prime minister Yitzhak Rabin, to a meeting held in the West Bank town of Ramallah on September 11, 1997. At this meeting, the two signed a document reaffirming the principles of the Oslo Accord reached four years earlier between Arafat and Prime Minister Rabin.

whom Israel had signed the agreement, would be solely responsible for acting against terrorists in the occupied territories. Israel had even supplied him with weapons to arm a police force. Since Israel would no longer be looking over Hamas's shoulder, so to speak, the terrorist organization could now prepare for its attacks without any fear that Israel would learn of the plans and quash them.

Yehiya Ayyash

It is not clear exactly how Hamas arrived at its decision to begin launching suicide attacks, but it is clear that the talents of one man, Yehiya Ayyash, greatly enhanced its ability to embark on this much more violent course of action. Known as the Engineer, Ayyash was the mastermind behind Hamas's foray into suicide bombing.

Ayyash did not fit the picture of the typical Hamas terrorist. He was well educated, ambitious, soft-spoken, and came from a relatively affluent family. He was married and had a child. After graduating from Birzeit University in the West Bank, where he had studied electrical engineering, Ayyash had planned to earn his master's degree. When Israeli authorities turned down his request for permission to study in Jordan, however, he became depressed and bitter. It was around this time that he became active in Hamas.

Ayyash had a genius for electronics and chemistry, and he harnessed this genius to invent what came to be known as his signature bomb. Using everyday, easily obtainable items, such as car batteries and carpenters' nails, he constructed a bomb that, upon explosion, would cause terrible damage to buildings and human bodies. Before Ayyash came on the scene, Hamas's explosive devices were extremely crude, consisting of pipes packed with hundreds of match heads. It had never before had access to such an effective and deadly weapon.

Planning a Suicide Attack

Once the decision to launch a suicide attack has been made, a number of operations must be performed. The target has to be selected, and intelligence must be gathered about the location's

The wreckage of an Israeli bus that exploded on October 19, 1994, in the middle of one of Tel Aviv's busiest streets. This Hamas suicide bombing, in which twenty-two people died, is thought to have been masterminded by the Palestinian extremist and explosions expert Yehiya Ayyash, also known as the Engineer. Israel accused him of sending seven suicide bombers on missions that killed at least fifty-five Israelis and wounded about three hundred.

layout and periods of peak activity, checkpoints that need to be crossed, transportation schedules, and so on. The bomber must be recruited and trained, both physically and spiritually. Finally, the bomb must be constructed, and plans and preparations for transporting the suicide bomber to the target area must be made.

A female Palestinian member of Hamas holds a Koran and a fake gun and wears an outfit typical of suicide bombers, including a headband that reads, "We love to be martyrs." Though typical Hamas suicide bombers used to be young, single, uneducated males, recent recruits have included middle-aged fathers and young female students. This broadening of the bomber profile seems to indicate that Palestinian anger and frustration have spread widely throughout the population.

Recruiting the Bomber

The task of recruiting Palestinian suicide bombers is carried out by al-Qassam operatives known as watchers, who search the mosques and Islamic learning centers for men they think might be willing to become suicide bombers. At the time of the 1994

The Tactical Advantages of Suicide Bombing

From a tactical standpoint, suicide bombing has many advantages over conventional terrorism, such as assassinations or kidnappings. It is simple and inexpensive. No escape routes or complicated rescue operations are required. And since the fear of consequences is more or less done away with, the suicide bomber has more freedom to choose the exact time, location, and circumstances of the attack. Since the attacker will almost certainly die in the explosion, the chance that captured and interrogated terrorists will reveal important information is eliminated.

attacks, the typical candidate would be a person who seemed to have no future and no hope for one. He would be unmarried and a loner, someone who had no job prospects and no chance of finding a wife. Today, Hamas seems to be drawing on a wider pool of recruits, including women, students, breadwinners, and middle-aged fathers.

After identifying a candidate, Hamas political officers embrace the potential bomber in public, usually inside a mosque or prayer center. This public display of affection is calculated to provide the suicide bomber with a sense of belonging and self-importance, something that someone who has grown up in a refugee camp or in an impoverished city on occupied land probably has rarely felt.

Once the candidate is "hooked" and his security check comes back clean, the idea of going on a suicide bombing mission is

Members of Hamas march through the Jabalya refugee camp in the Gaza Strip carrying makeshift mortars and grenade launchers in April 2001. The demonstrators wave banners that read, "Security coordination is a betrayal," referring to joint Palestinian and Israeli attempts to fight terrorism in the West Bank and Gaza Strip. The masked men with fake explosives strapped around their waists wear signs that label them as "martyrs-in-waiting."

proposed to him. The rewards of such a mission are described to him in detail. For example, "martyrs" are promised a harem of dozens of beautiful wives in Paradise and a place of honor near Allah and his prophets. Their families are promised financial comfort and high social standing.

Preparing the Bomber

Hamas selects a would-be bomber for his mission just days, and sometimes only hours, before it is scheduled to occur (until recently, all Hamas suicide bombers were male). He is not allowed to say good-bye to his family or tell them of his plans. In order to prepare the recruit emotionally and psychologically for his mission, Hamas members dress him in the white, hooded shroud that is usually used to cover dead bodies for burial. Then they take him to a cemetery, where he is told to prepare for death by lying between gravesites for several hours.

After this "funeral" ritual, he is taken to a safe house, where a video is made of him in which he proclaims his devotion to Islam and affirms his commitment to becoming a suicide bomber. At this time a still photograph is also taken of him. This photograph, along with photos of the carnage that result from his mission, is later used as part of his "martyrdom poster," which is reproduced and displayed throughout the Palestinian territories.

Once at the target site, the recruit is told to remain calm and blend in with the crowd as much as possible. He is told to wait until he is surrounded by as many Israeli civilians as possible before pressing the switch to explode the bomb, in order to ensure that maximum casualties will result.

The Cycle
of Violence

Holocaust Remembrance Day is a national day of mourning in Israel. At 11:00 AM, air-raid sirens sound throughout the country, and everyone stops whatever they are doing and stands in silence, with their heads bowed, in a moment of reflection, honoring the six million Jews who were killed in the Holocaust. It is the first of three annual celebrations designed to pay tribute to the victims of the Holocaust and to celebrate the creation of Israel.

It was on the eve of this most solemn of days, in 1994, that Hamas chose to unleash its new and devastating terrorist weapon—the suicide bomber—on the people of Israel.

The Attack

At 12:15 PM, on April 6, 1994, the day before Holocaust Remembrance Day, a nineteen-year-old Palestinian Hamas member pulled into a busy intersection in the center of Afula, a small city in the Jezreel Valley of northern Israel. The streets were crowded with Israeli high school students who had been let out early because of the coming holiday.

As a group of students boarded the number 348 bus, the bomber drove a stolen 1987 sky blue Opel Ascona in front of the bus, cutting it off. In the trunk was a bomb consisting of seven gas cylinders hooked to an explosive charge of five antipersonnel hand grenades, surrounded by a backpack containing nails. The suicide bomber pressed a detonation switch positioned alongside the driver's side door, exploding the Opel. The blast spread intense heat, flames, and shredded metal over a forty-yard radius, resulting in eight deaths and forty-four serious injuries.

Hours after the Afula blast, special crews of rabbis (Jewish religious leaders and teachers) scoured the nearby roadside for bits and pieces of the victims. It is a common practice in Israel for rabbis to visit the scenes of terrorist attacks to gather up the remains of the victims. According to Judaism, the human body is sacred in death as well as in life, and it must be given proper burial.

The Hunt for Ayyash

In the meantime, Israeli secret police had identified Yehiya Ayyash as the mastermind of the Afula suicide bombing. An elaborate manhunt for Ayyash ensued. Photos of him hung at every military checkpoint in the West Bank, and his picture was printed in numerous Israeli newspapers.

Though Ayyash was considered a murderer and an outlaw in Israel, he became a hero to the Palestinian people. Parents named their sons after him; women embroidered his picture onto table-cloths; folksongs were written about him. For two years the Israeli secret police searched for him, with no success. During this time he traveled through the occupied territories, going from safe house to safe house, disguising himself as an old man or woman, and even as a Jewish settler.

Mourners carry the coffin bearing the remains of 30-year-old Yehiya Ayyash through Gaza City during the funeral procession on January 6, 1996. Thousands of angry Palestinians vowed revenge for his assassination at the hands of Israeli agents and urged Israel to "prepare the body bags." Inset: Ayyash, who was killed on January 5, 1996, in the Gaza Strip town of Beit Lahia.

Israeli police would conduct weekly searches of his family home. There they would find notes from Ayyash to his family and photographs of Ayyash clutching his son with one hand and an assault rifle with the other. Somehow or other Ayyash managed to make frequent, secretive visits to his wife and family during the manhunt. It was during this period that his wife became pregnant with their second child.

Finally, after two years of searching for him, Israeli agents managed to put a trace on Ayyash's cellular phone and were able to track him through the radio signals the phone emitted.

Ayyash's Assassination

Negotiating their way through networks of Palestinian informers and collaborators, the Israeli police were finally able to develop a controversial plan that they hoped would put a quick end to suicide bombings: the assassination of Yehiya Ayyash. Israeli agents scrambled Ayyash's cellular phone line, making him think his phone was broken. When Ayyash brought it in for repair, he was given a replacement cell phone rigged with explosives.

At nine o'clock on the morning of January 5, 1996, the cell phone rang at the home of Osama Hamad, where Ayyash had been hiding out for months. "I went up to his room, woke him up, and handed him the phone," said Hamad, a twenty-seven-year-old Hamas activist in an interview with the *St. Louis Post-Dispatch*. "He started talking to his father. I walked away to let him speak privately," Hamad said. "Suddenly I heard the explosion and looked back and saw smoke. I looked around for Yehiya. Then I saw him. He was decapitated." The explosives were activated when the signal was received that Ayyash was on the line. Phone lines to the hideout had been cut off to force Ayyash to use the mobile phone.

Hamas vowed to avenge Ayyash's death. Within a period of eight days in February and March of 1996, it launched a series of six terrorist attacks, killing sixty Israelis.

Hamas Overturns Israeli Elections

In the period just before the 1996 bombings, most Israelis had been in favor of seeking peace with the Palestinians, even if it meant giving up land. There had been a lull in Hamas terrorism, and as a consequence Israelis began to believe that it might be possible to coexist as friendly neighbors with Palestinians. But the Hamas bombings quickly eroded support for a peace deal and any future concessions with the Palestinians. In direct response to the bombings, Israeli prime minister Shimon Peres, Yitzhak Rabin's successor, called a halt to the peace talks (in 1995 Prime Minister Rabin had been assassinated by a far-right-wing Israeli who objected to Rabin's peace overtures).

In addition to the collapse of peace talks, the 1996 bombings also led to the defeat of Peres, who was a member of the left-wing Labor Party (the Israeli party generally most willing to seek a negotiated settlement with the Palestinians). Israelis did not feel that Peres, who had been instrumental in negotiating the Oslo peace accord that earned him the 1994 Nobel Peace Prize together with Arafat and Rabin, was strong enough to protect them from radical Palestinian militants. In 1996 they replaced him with Benjamin Netanyahu, a member of the right-wing Likud Party, who vowed to be tough on terrorism.

Rescue workers inspect a damaged hotel banquet room in the Israeli seaside resort of Netanya on March 27, 2002, following an attack that killed at least twenty-two Israelis. The suicide bombing occurred in a crowded dining room at the Park Hotel, a coastal resort, during the traditional meal marking the start of Passover. Hamas claimed responsibility for the attack.

A Future Without Fear?

In May 2000, Israeli artists and Palestinian youths worked together to paint a mural on a wall in a Palestinian refugee camp. In Arabic and Hebrew, they painted "A Future Without Fear." That was before the current intifada, which began in September 2000 and intensified with a relentless wave of suicide bombings and harsh Israeli reprisals in early 2002. After the intifada began, residents of the Palestinian camp tore down the wall, rebuilt it, and painted a new slogan: "One Choice—to Return or to Die," referring to the refugees' desire to return to the land Israel considers its own.

In February 2001, a prime minister even less willing to negotiate with the Palestinians than Netanyahu was voted in: Ariel Sharon. Under his administration, peace talks would break down completely. An even more violent and relentless wave of suicide bombings was unleashed by Hamas, leading to an overpowering military response by the Israeli army that leveled whole towns in the Palestinian territories. Over 300 Israelis were killed in suicide attacks between September 2000 and April 2002 (including five American students following an attack upon Hebrew University in Jerusalem), while estimates of the Palestinian casualties resulting from the Israeli response range from several dozen to several hundred, depending on who is asked. Among those killed was prominent Hamas military commander Sheikh Salah Shehada, who died during an Israeli airstrike on a crowded Gaza City residential neighborhood. Despite American attempts to arrange a cease-fire and bring both sides back to the negotiating table, peace never seemed further away than it did in the war-torn spring of 2002.

Conclusion

ccording to opinion polls conducted at the end of 2001, 70 percent of Palestinians currently favor suicide bombings and oppose a cease-fire. Most Palestinians think that terrorism is a reasonable way to pressure the Israelis to withdraw from the West Bank and Gaza Strip. Many Palestinians do not consider Hamas members terrorists; they instead think of them as liberators.

And it is true that for many Palestinians, the suicide bombers are heroes. In the territories, people speak with admiration about the "martyrs." Schoolchildren are asked to write compositions in praise of dead militants. Palestinian towns and villages are filled with martyrdom posters that celebrate their valiant deeds. Indeed, for a population of people whose lives are marked by poverty and despair, the suicide bombers offer a measure of dignity and self-respect and a feeling of power. Through the suicide bombers, ordinary Palestinians feel they are exercising some control over their destiny.

Voices for Peace

Despite the fact that so many Palestinians support Hamas's terrorist activities, however, there are those who recognize the fact that violence does not serve them well at all. "It's not good, these attacks that the Palestinians are doing," a pregnant Palestinian mother of four is quoted as saying in the *New York Times Magazine*. "It only brings Israeli retaliation."

Palestinian militants wave Hamas flags as they surround their spiritual leader, Sheikh Ahmed Yassin, seated in the car. The April 2002 rally in the Jabalya refugee camp was a protest against Israel's recent military offensive there. During the rally, Sheikh Yassin urged Palestinians to continue the intifada and promised that Yasir Arafat would never surrender to Israeli forces.

In the same article, Ahmad Abu Salem, a Palestinian truck driver, agrees. He says that it is in the interest of the people for the violence to stop. "We are the ones paying a heavy price. We are hungry. We are unemployed. We are . . . injured in the cross fire."

"It's about meals on the table," says another Palestinian, a man who makes his living as a cab driver in Israel. "Hamas doesn't care if we have meals on the table."

There are even those who go so far as to question the heroism of the suicide bombers. "Excuse me . . . what did they do, these noble creatures?" asks one Palestinian in the *Times Magazine* article. "Blow themselves up? They blew themselves up and blew us up with them. To hell with them."

Israeli Views

The majority of Israelis, too, feel hopeless about any possibility for peace with the Palestinians. Pointing to Yasir Arafat's promise to stop terrorism in exchange for the land that Israel acquired during the 1967 war, they ask: Why did they attack us in the first place, if all they want now is for Israel to return the land? How do we know they won't try to destroy us again once we return the land?

They say that instead of fighting terrorism, Yasir Arafat secretly supports it. They point to his refusal to delete a clause in the PLO Charter that calls for the removal of the "Zionist presence from Palestine." They point to a speech he made before an Arab audience in which he indicated that making peace with Israel is just a ploy, a means to an end. In addition, the Israeli government has released documents, confiscated during the 2002 incursions into Palestinian territory, that it claims prove Arafat funnels money from his political party to terrorists for the purchase of weapons and bomb-making materials.

In the face of almost daily acts of violence, more and more Israelis favor reprisals of the harshest kind. The army's violent and destructive antiterrorist sweeps into Palestinian territory in the spring of 2002 received overwhelming public support. Every act of terrorism makes a compromise between Israel and the Palestinians seem less likely. Israelis are afraid to live next to a state that seems as if it is ruled by terrorists. As one Israeli observer puts it, "How would you like it if Osama bin Laden had a state, and it was next to your state?"

A majority of Israelis support the government's strategy of assassinating key Palestinian militants. Some even want a permanent occupation of Palestinian territories. At protest rallies staged on the site of terrorist attacks, some Israelis wearing T-shirts that read "No Arabs—No Attacks," chant "Death to Arabs!" At the same rallies, however, there are also those who hold up signs that read "Revenge Equals Continuing the Cycle of Blood."

The thirst for revenge does not run very deep in the heart of the Israeli people, says Nira Chadad, an Israeli art student who was interviewed at the site of a recent terrorist attack. "That's just the heat of the moment," she told the *Guardian*. "It's instinctive to call for death to Arabs. After something like this, people always go crazy, but it's not their real feeling."

Whatever their political point of view, almost every Israeli has a deep desire to live in peace. And despite all the complexities of the situation, when viewed from a certain perspective, this does not seem like it should be so much to ask.

"If you look at a map you will see that Israel is so small. It's smaller than New Jersey," says Sarah Shapiro. "It's so small that on the map its name can't fit on it. It's always out on the Mediterranean because it won't fit. It's surrounded by Arab countries, but Hamas can't bear to have any Jews there. They think that speaking of peace with Israel is a renunciation of Arab values.

"We would love to work together in peace," she says. "Jews don't have a natural hatred for Arabs. It's not in our bones to hate them. All we want to do is live in this place where our history started."

Glossary

agenda   An underlying plan or program; what one wants to achieve.

cache   A hiding place for concealing and preserving provisions or weapons.

cease-fire   A period during a war when both sides agree to stop fighting.

contend   To strive against a rival or against difficulties.

escalate   To increase in extent, volume, number, amount, intensity, or scope.

guerrilla   A member of a small group of amateur, volunteer fighters who attack an organized army.

infidel   An unbeliever with respect to a particular religion.

intifada   In Arabic, "shaking off"; an uprising.

Islam   A religion that is based on the teachings of the religion's founder, Mohammed.

martyr   One who chooses to suffer death in order to further a belief, cause, principle, or religious faith.

militant   A person who is willing to take up arms to support a belief or political cause.

Muslim   A person whose religion is Islam.

Palestine Liberation Organization (PLO)   Created in 1964 and led by Yasir Arafat, this group hopes to liberate the Gaza Strip, the West Bank, and Jerusalem from Israeli rule. The organization also wants to form an independent Palestinian state. Formerly a terrorist organization, now considered a legitimate political party.

peace treaty   A formal agreement between two or more countries promising that the countries will not wage war against each other.

shrine   A building or place that is considered holy by a religious group. A shrine can contain holy objects or be the site of an important past religious event.

suicide bomber   A terrorist who blows himself or herself up with a bomb in order to kill other people who are considered the enemy.

United Nations (UN)   An international organization headquartered in New York City. It includes representatives from most countries and helps promote international peace, security, and economic development.

Zionism   An international movement created in the 1890s that was originally committed to the establishment of a Jewish national homeland in Palestine. Since 1948, it has been dedicated to the support, defense, and preservation of the modern state of Israel.

For More Information

Central Intelligence Agency (CIA)
Office of Public Affairs
Washington, DC 20505
(703) 482-0623
Web site: http://www.cia.gov

Council on American-Islamic Relations (CAIR)
453 New Jersey Avenue SE
Washington, DC 20003-4034
(202) 488-8787
Web site: http://www.cair-net.org

Federal Bureau of Investigation (FBI)
J. Edgar Hoover Building
935 Pennsylvania Avenue NW
Washington, DC 20535-0001
(202) 324-3000
Web site: http://www.fbi.gov

Federation of American Scientists (FAS)
Intelligence Resource Program
1717 K Street NW, Suite 209
Washington, DC 20036
(202) 454-4691
Web site: http://www.fas.org/irp/index.html

National Security Agency (NSA)
Public Affairs Office
9800 Savage Road
Fort George G. Meade, MD 20755-6779
(301) 688-6524
Web site: http://www.nsa.gov

National Security Institute (NSI)
116 Main Street, Suite 200
Medway, MA 02053
(508) 533-9099
Web site: http://nsi.org

Terrorist Group Profiles
Dudley Knox Library
Naval Postgraduate School
411 Dyer Road
Monterey, CA 93943
Web site: http://library.nps.navy.mil/home/

Web Sites

Due to the changing nature of Internet links, the Rosen
Publishing Group, Inc., has developed an online list of Web sites
related to the subject of this book. This site is updated regularly.
Please use this link to access the list:

http://www.rosenlinks.com/iwmito/hama/

For Further Reading

Altman, Linda Jacobs. *The Creation of Israel.* San Diego, CA: Lucent Books, 1998.

Anita, Ganeri. *I Remember Palestine.* Minneapolis, MN: Econo-Clad Books, 1999.

Gordon, Matthew S. *Islam.* New York: Facts on File, 1991.

Hamilton, Josh. *Behind the Terror.* Minneapolis, MN: Abdo and Daughters, 2002.

Holliday, Laurel. *Why Do They Hate Me?* Minneapolis, MN: Econo-Clad Books, 2000.

Ousseimi, Maria. *Caught in the Crossfire.* New York: Walker & Co., 1995.

Schlesinger, Arthur M., ed. *Jerusalem and the Holy Land: Chronicles from National Geographic.* New York: Chelsea House, 1999.

Schroeter, Daniel J. *Israel: An Illustrated History.* New York: Oxford University Press Children's Books, 1999.

Spencer, William. *Islamic Fundamentalism and the Modern World.* Brookfield, CT: Millbrook Press, 1995.

Wagner, Heather Lehr. *Israel and the Arab World.* New York: Chelsea House, 2002.

Bibliography

"Bush Freezes Assets of Charity Tie to Hamas." Online NewsHour. December 4, 2001. Retrieved March 2002 (http://www.pbs.org/newshour/updates/december01/hamas_12-4.html).

Cohn-Sherbok, Dan, and Dawoud el-Alami. *The Palestine-Israeli Conflict.* Oxford, England: Oneworld Publications Ltd., 2001.

Goldenberg, Suzanne, and Virginia Quirke. "Israelis United by Desire For Revenge." *Guardian Unlimited.* August 10, 2001. Retrieved March 2002 (http://www.guardian.co.uk/Archive/Article/0,4273,4236806,00.html).

Hass, Amira. *Drinking the Sea At Gaza: Days and Nights In a Land Under Seige.* New York: Owl Books, 2000.

Hiro, Dilip. *Sharing the Promised Land.* New York: Olive Branch Press, 1999.

Kass, Jeffrey H. "Palestinians Should Meet Terms of Accords." *St. Louis Post-Dispatch.* June 8, 1996.

Katz, Samuel M. *The Hunt for the Engineer: How Israeli Agents Tracked the Hamas Master Bomber.* New York: Fromm International, 1999.

Kelley, Jack. "Devotion, Desire, Drive Youths to 'Martyrdom.'" *USA Today.* July 5, 2001.

Laquer, Walter, and Barry Rubin, eds. *The Israel-Arab Reader: A Documentary History of the Middle East Conflict.* New York: Penguin USA, 2001.

Lesch, Ann M., and Dan Tschirgi. *Origins and Development of the Arab-Israeli Conflict.* New York: Greenwood Press, 1998.

Mishal, Shaul, and Avraham Sela. *The Palestinian Hamas.* New York: Columbia University Press, 2000.

Morris, Benny. *Righteous Victims: A History of the Zionist-Arab Conflict, 1881–1999.* New York: Alfred A. Knopf, Inc., 2001.

Nusse, Andrea. *Muslim Palestine: The Ideology of Hamas.* New York: Routledge, 1998.

Peters, Joan. *From Time Immemorial: The Origins of the Arab-Jewish Conflict over Palestine.* Chicago: JKAP Publications, 2001.

Radin, Charles A. "Hamas Children Raised to Fight, Die. Terrorist Group Won't Accept Israel." *Boston Globe.* December 26, 2001.

Remnick, David. "Letter from Jerusalem." *The New Yorker.* January 7, 2002.

Sachor, Howard M. *A History of Israel: From the Rise of Zionism to Our Time.* New York: Alfred A. Knopf, Inc., 1996.

Shapiro, Sarah, interview with author, New York, New York, March 2, 2002.

Sivan, Emmanuel. "How Strong is Hamas?" *Newsweek.* December 7, 2002.

Smith, Charles D. *Palestine and the Arab-Israeli Conflict.* New York: Bedford/St. Martins Press, 2001.

Sontag, Susan. "The Palestinian Conversation." *The New York Times Magazine.* February 3, 2002.

Warner, Margaret. "Critical Moment: Palestine." Online NewsHour. June 4, 2001. Retrieved March 2002 (http://www.pbs.org/newshour/bb/middle_east/jan-june01/rahman_6-4.html).

Index

I

intifada, 16–18, 19, 30, 49
Iraq, 12
Islam, 16, 21, 41
Israel
    history of, 8–14
    retaliation for suicide bombings, 7,
        22–23, 49, 50, 52, 53
    settlement of by Jews, 14
Israelis
    precautions taken by, 4
    views of, 52–53
Izzdine al Qassam Brigade, 19, 31, 38

J

Jerusalem, 4, 8, 12, 14, 16, 26
    East Jerusalem, 14, 16, 26
jihad, 18
Jordan, 12, 13, 36

K

King Solomon's Temple, 12, 16
Koran, 21

L

Lebanon, 12, 22
Lebanon War (1982), 22

M

martyrdom, 18, 26, 29, 31, 40, 41, 50
Mohammed (prophet), 16
Moses, 16

N

Netanyahu, Benjamin, 47, 49
New City (Jerusalem), 12

O

occupied territories, 14, 49
Old City (Jerusalem), 12
Oslo Accords, 34–35, 47

P

Palestine, history of, 8–14
Palestine Liberation Organization (PLO),
    16, 18, 21, 22, 52
Palestinians
    how they view suicide bombings, 26,
        29, 50–52
    restrictions put on by Israel, 21
peace talks, 22, 34–35, 47, 49, 53
Peres, Shimon, 47

R

Rabin, Yitzhak, 34, 47
Rahman, Hasan Abdel, 21
refugee camps, 7, 20, 39, 49

S

Salem, Ahmad Abu, 51
Saudi Arabia, 12
Sbarro pizzeria bombing (2001), 24–25, 26
September 11, 2001, terrorist attacks, 30
Shaked, Roni, 28
Shapiro, Sarah, 4, 24, 53
Sharon, Ariel, 49
Shin Bet (Israeli secret police), 19, 43
Sinai Campaign (1956), 22
Sinai Peninsula, 14, 22
Six Day War (1967), 13–15
Suez Canal, 22
suicide bombing, 4, 30
    in Afula (1994), 24, 42–43
    children groomed for, 26, 28–29

Index

families of bombers, 29, 31, 40
how bombers are viewed, 26, 29, 50–52
how it became a tactic, 32, 36
planning of, 36–37
preparing bombers, 31, 41
recruiting bombers, 38–40
of Sbarro pizzeria (2001), 24–25
tactical advantages of, 39
in 2002, 22, 49
Syria, 12, 13, 22

T

truces, 22

U

United Nations, 9, 12, 22
    resolution on Israel, 9, 12, 34

W

Wailing Wall, 16
West Bank, 19, 21, 22, 26, 29, 36, 43, 50

annexed by Jordan, 12
acquired by Israel, 14
massacre at Hebron, 32
PLO in, 18
settlement of by Jews, 15
Western Wall, 12, 16

Y

Yassin, Ahmed, 19
Yemen, 12
Yom Kippur War (1973), 22
Yosef, Sheik Hasan, 26

Z

Zaqarna, Ra'id, 42–43
Zionism, 8, 9, 29, 52

About the Author

Maxine Rosaler is a freelance writer who lives in New York City.

Photo Credits

Series Design and Layout

Nelson Sá